Peace in the Morning

Images and Meditations to Begin Your Day

Photographs by Daniel B. Ford Jr.

Meditations by Father Hal Helms

PARACLETE PRESS
BREWSTER, MASSACHUSETTS

2021 First Printing

Peace in the Morning: Images and Meditations to Begin Your Day
Copyright © 2021 by Daniel B. Ford, Jr. and The Community of Jesus
ISBN 978-1-64060-717-0
Library of Congress Control Number: 2021939196
The Paraclete Press name and logo (dove on cross) are trademarks of Paraclete Press.

10 9 8 7 6 5 4 3 2 1

Published by Paraclete Press
Brewster, Massachusetts
www.paracletepress.com

Printed in Korea by Prinpia Co., Ltd.

Contents

INTRODUCTION

Beauty brings with it peace and joy. And beauty, I have discovered, is all around us.

On the most difficult of days, I am usually able to walk outside and see something beautiful. Over the years, I've learned to capture these moments with my camera. It is these images of beauty that I offer you here, in the hope that you'll use them to find your own beautiful places and spaces in this world.

There is a world to come that will be beautiful beyond all our imagining. I believe that with all my being. But I also believe this world—where we are right now—is full of what should fill us with the wonder of God, who is Beauty itself.

When I was a child I would crop scenes in my mind by selecting a beautiful area to observe and then imaginatively removing from the scene whatever it was I thought distracted from its essential beauty.

As I became older, I was introduced to my first camera. This was many decades ago when we only had black and white film. Then I realized that I'd been doing photography before I even knew to call it that.

My interest in photography developed, early on, into what photographers would call *contrast*: the visual ratio among different tones of white, black, and gray, and the ways they contrast with each other in a visual field. I was mostly unaware of color in those early days of taking pictures. I even resisted color film, for a time, because I was so drawn to contrast. I thought then that stunning tonal contrasts, combined with my ideas of composition, were all there was to seeing and appreciating beauty.

I mention this because much later in life—in my late sixties—I was urged to take painting lessons. Why? I wondered at first. And then I responded, *No way, I like photographs. I don't care about colors. I probably couldn't even name the primary colors. Why would I want to paint?*

Now, more than ten years later, I'm having the time of my life painting with oils: copying—exactly copying—some of my enlarged photographs. Admittedly, that's something a talented monkey could probably manage. But, as I see it, there is no way to improve on the beauty of an excellent scene created by God. Realism is fine with me, no matter the medium.

So, with this explanation of my approach to photography, you have a context for "entering into" the images that I offer in this little book.

Over a lifetime I have gone from black and white photography to oil paintings to color photography, all without deviating from finding peace and joy in capturing the Beauty of God. This is something available to all of us, if we just look for it. May your looking for it in these pages lead you to look for it all around you, wherever you are.

But I didn't want to simply offer you colorful images. I wanted to pair my images with passages of spiritual teaching from an old friend and mentor of mine, Father Hal Helms, who wrote a powerful book many years ago, also published by Paraclete Press, called *Echoes of Eternity*. I have chosen quotes from this work to pair with each of my photographs. Hal Helms was a pastor I loved and admired, a truly remarkable man who died at a relatively young age. His book has impacted the lives of tens of thousands of people; may these passages from Father Hal's writings lead you to discover more from him, as well.

I wish you peace in the morning.

CONSIDER

Interruptions are also of Me.

Do not forget the parable of the priest and the Levite. Never let your predetermined agenda keep you from seeing My hand in the interruption. It is there, whether you recognize it or not.

Mine indeed are the sheltering arms of love. Although you cannot see or recognize them, they are there. Faith, the faith that moves mountains and opens closed doors, sees them and rejoices.

My child, your
thankfulness
gladdens
My heart and
strengthens yours.

C all upon Me more faithfully and fervently, not for My sake but for yours. I know your needs and I am at work to meet them. . . . Beware of the stress of busyness that crowds out the call to turn aside to be with Me.

P ut away ill will.
It corrodes and eats away the
very foundation of your soul. You
cannot hate and really pray for
someone's good at the same time.

Think not that I have forgotten those for whom you pray. Let My love flow through your prayers to bless. My love waits, and in the meantime, I call you to believe, to expect, to love, and to pray.

Only in Me, My child,
is your true home
and goal.

Journey on.

My dear child, My word to you today is this: Walk in My love, as I have loved you. My love lays down a safe path for your feet. You do not know the dangers that surround you on every side, but I chart a safe course through them, and bid you walk there. The path is clear, and will open moment by moment as you have need.

I am the Lord your God.
Look for Me in all that
comes to pass today.

New every morning is My love for you. Let your love for Me be renewed in this meeting. Put the fears and shadows of the night behind you, and see Me in the unfolding of the day.

Behind the clouds, My glorious light. Behind the doubts, My sure promises. Behind the fears, My blessed hope.

Let no darkness remain in your soul, My child. Let the light of My Spirit shine in its hidden places.

Do not be content, My child, with the polluted waters of this present age. Turn your mind to My word of truth, My Shepherd's voice, and I will give you an abundance you have never dreamed possible. Seek the living water and be renewed.

PRAY

Happy are those who are invited to the marriage supper of the Lamb—a foretaste of that glory I give to My children in quiet moments of fellowship with Me. I have promised, and My promises are yea and amen. I will come in and sup with them and they with me.

Enter into the joy of your Lord. Not just at the end of the journey, My child, but even now, amid the shadows and rough places of the road, there is joy for you if you will abandon the burden of sadness. Enter into My joy, My beloved.

Truth is a spring of living water. It does not grow stale nor hackneyed, even though the verbal expressions may seem time-worn. Truth carries life-giving properties for the soul, and without these properties the soul languishes and shrivels. Cherish and hunger for truth, My child, for it shall make you free. Whether it be pleasant or bitter, its effect is health-bringing.

41

Faith still moves mountains—faith and prayer. This is what you need to practice: faith-filled praying—expectant, eager and confident praying. My heart is gladdened when My children pray this way. Don't be afraid of believing too much.

I tell you again that I have loved you with an everlasting love. When fear and darkness come upon you, recall this word to your mind. Resist the accusations of the adversary that My grace is not sufficient for your needs. Oh, there is plenteous grace beyond your direst need. Am I not God? Let love cross out fear and be one of those who find their delight in Me.

My goodness has never failed, the stream of mercy has never run dry. You have been fed with "the finest wheat" and you have been spared many sorrows. Forget not, My child, the signs I have given you of My loving care.

I am that Solid Rock. There is no other besides Me. O my dear child, I am so much greater than these little "chunks" of opinion you stand on so bravely and full of pride. Your rightness is not your salvation. I am your salvation.

My power and love will combine
and My glory will be shown.
Awaken your heart, be expectant,
not reluctant, before My promise.

51

I invite you, My child, into
My light. Where
I am, there is light.

O My dear child, the wonders of My love encompass you on every side. Why are you afraid to look more deeply? Do you not yet know that My intention for you is love? I, the Lord, appeal to you: trust Me and do not separate yourself from the fullness of My love.

My child, My child, your prayer is heard. I do not despise you in your need. I know your frame and am acquainted with all your ways. I want you to draw near to Me and keep fellowship with Me. I want you to know that I am always with you, even when you are least aware of My presence. I am not a God who is far off, but One who is near.

My child, today is a gift of My love. Your very life is a gift of My love for you. I want you to live as a child of love. I want you to reflect that love in your relations with others. Since I am the Source and Giver of life, there is no shortage of supply. Make the day brighter around you by denying your darkness and letting My light shine through you.

I go before you, My child, and prepare the way. When you walk in My way, your life fulfills My purpose for you. These days have been given for purposes you cannot fully see nor understand. Yours is not to view the distant scene, but to stay close to Me and let My will prevail.

Your knowledge of Me is grounded in My dealings with you. I am mindful of you, even when you are not mindful of Me. I am at work in the circumstances and consciences of those for whom you pray. You do not yet realize the power of prayer nor its place in My universe. As you obey My Spirit you come to a fuller, firmer knowledge of Me, and are blessed. I am ever mindful of you, My child.

Your prayers are heard, My child, and you need not fear. Hold fast to what you know, to My dealings and the revealings of My heart to you. These are steady lodestars by which to chart your course. You need not fear what lies ahead, because I always prepare the way for you. When you walk with Me, no harm can come to you.

LOOK

Yes, My child, you have been snatched from the jaws of death more times than you can possibly know. I have been with you and you knew it not. My patience and My lovingkindness have been your salvation.

Today I call you to accept and enjoy My merciful presence. I am with you, My child, so do not ignore My lovingkindness.

69

Blessed indeed are you, My child, to be called into the fellowship of the redeemed. Happy, thrice happy, are those who forsake their ways and follow Me.

My dear child,
I delight in those
who find their
delight in Me.

Take My burden in place of yours. My burden of care, of love for others who may never return yours in kind, of faithfulness in prayer and the burden of faith, of believing where you cannot see. Accept this burden, My child, and travel light!

I have not called you to walk a blind path, even though the future is unknown to you. I have called you to walk with Me, and I tell you again, I am enough—sufficient for any circumstance you are called to face. No exceptions!

My light is ever shining. It is always available to My children. I do not withhold it from those who are willing to seek it and walk in it. So choose light rather than darkness. Choose life rather than death. Choose My peace rather than torment. You are blessed when your mind is stayed on Me.

With My peace I bless those who seek it. It is found in unexpected places and times, for it is not a peace as the world knows it. My peace is found in surrender. To the extent that you agree with My will, you realize that peace. It may be in the midst of uncertainty, even of pain, but when your will is united with Mine, peace follows.

Great peace have they who love My way.

Remember always, My child, I seek your good. My will for you is good. Despise not My ways, for they are the Way to life, peace, hope, and joy.

As My love and My ever-new mercies operate in your life and the life of your loved ones, learn to entrust them and yourself to My tender care. Only then can you know the "peace that passes understanding." For your peace will not depend on your understanding.

My gift to you is My indwelling Spirit. With no conscious awareness on your part, I dwell within, because you have been sealed unto the Day of redemption. I am gathering unto Myself a people to dwell eternally with Me. Even now that dwelling is prepared, and your life span is preparation to fit you for it. By My Spirit's indwelling, a work of training, pruning, cleansing, and nourishing is going on in your soul, so that when I raise you up, you will be prepared for the joys I have prepared.

By streams of living water, I lead you, My child. Thirsty and faint, you will find refreshment here. I am that water which gives new life, renewed vigor, and fresh beauty to your soul. The waters of comfort are here.

The cleansing of sin is here. Do not fear to see and recognize My uses of material water to convey the blessing of living water. Stoop down, and drink, and live.

My light brings life, even as it discloses the distortions and deformities that must be healed. I am He who makes the crooked straight, the Healing of that which is out of joint. My light and truth belong to the Day of My coming, and I call you to be a child of the Day.

My dear child, do not forget that I love you. Do not heedlessly trample on My love by doubting it or forgetting it. My love is a purifier of motives, the inner hidden workings of the heart. Everything that I ask of you and everything that I allow to come into your life is rooted in My divine love. You cannot measure or understand or comprehend My love—but you can accept it in a way you never have.

I make the light of My countenance to shine upon you. I look upon you with mercy and compassion, because I know who you are. Look on yourself not with disdain or despising. You are the work of My hands. The light of My countenance still shines upon you, and the path before us still leads to your true destiny.

97

My word to you today is: Stay.
Stay on the course I have laid out for you.
Stay your mind and thoughts on Me.

Draw near to Me, My child, and I will not fail to draw near to you. You never seek Me in vain, no matter what your feelings tell you. I, the Lord, change not. My face is ever toward you for good even when you are least aware of it.

DRAW NEAR TO ME

My dear child, My thoughts are not like your thoughts, and My ways are not like your ways. I counsel you to listen, to pray, and to refuse to retreat into a stronghold of righteousness. Only in this way can you allow the truth further entrance into your soul. Only in this way can your thoughts align themselves with Mine. That, My dear child, is My aim and desire for you.

LIVE

I call you to center your heart upon Me. Your failures and successes are not the goal of life. The true goal is to seek and find true life in Me.

Do you not know, My child, that I am the Source and Giver of the peace for which you long? Seek that peace which is Mine, for in it you will be freed from the night demons of panic and terror. Claim the inheritance which is yours as My child, and do not despise My dealings. Let not your heart be troubled, neither let it be afraid.

I still choose to speak in the "still, small voice" rather in than the thunder. My yoke is easy. I am gentle and lowly of heart. But because I love you and care for your welfare, I will speak in thunder if necessary. So tune your heart to hear. Be assured that the Voice is there, and that it is possible to commune with Me more consistently than you have ever known.

It is My delight to s

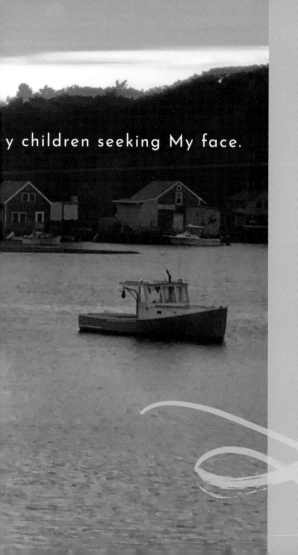

y children seeking My face.

Seek and you shall find. Knock and it shall be opened to you. I am found by those who seek, ask, look—and I never turn away any sincere soul.

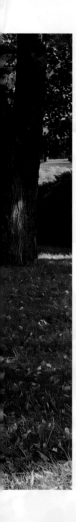

I am truth and I am life. The words that I speak to you come with the nature of Truth. Never fear truth, My child, for it is life-giving and healing, even when it is most painful. Deception and delusions are ever ready to bend or twist the truth so as to destroy its effectiveness. Remember this: deception is death-dealing; truth is life-bringing. The song and the joy in your heart must always be grounded in the truth. Open your heart, then, to My truth and My life.

want to see more joy, more faith,
more freedom in My children.
I want you all to rejoice in your
salvation which has been achieved
at so great a price. As long as
you allow fear and foreboding to
prevail, you refuse the abundant
life I have given you. Obedience
and joy must kiss each other. Put
off the old garment of doubt and
put on the new garment of joy
and praise.

Hear, My child, the word for today. There is no need that I cannot fill. There is no situation that I cannot redeem. Only by trusting Me beyond the limits of your reasoning can you begin to have freedom from the plaguing fears.

As the morning light rises in the dawn, illuminating the waiting earth, so My light rises in the soul, quietly, gently illuminating the inner heart. Do not shrink from My light, My child, for without it you are doomed to dwell in darkness. I am He who makes the crooked straight, the Healing of that which is out of joint. My light and truth belong to the Day of My coming, and I call you to be a child of the Day.

Have no fear for
tomorrow, My child.
Tomorrow will hold only
what I bring or allow
in your life. All your
tomorrows are in My
hand. I am the Lord of
the years. My hand is a
gracious hand and all My
ways are faithfulness.

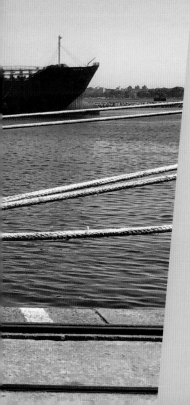

My will is peace.
Peace amid strife and
peace growing out of strife.

I will walk with you, My child, all the way. I do not forsake those who put their trust in Me, however weak and wavering their faith may be.

Put away this faithless fear you have been entertaining. I will be with you. What is there to fear with Me at hand? I repeat again: there is nothing to fear with Me at hand.

I am with you in your struggle against your fallen nature. I have redeemed you. I have called you by name. You are Mine.

Expect good—that is the faith that moves mountains. That is the faith that unlocks closed doors. That is the faith that overcomes the world. Simple? Yes, My child, for your life turns on such simple truth. You bring your needs, knowing from all your past experiences that My help does not fail.

If you will listen more carefully and obey more readily, you will not be terrified by the billows and waves of life. Keep faith with this secret place. Again I say, Keep faith!

Draw near to Me, and I will draw near to you. I am ever near, but you are usually unmindful of it. It takes a conscious choice on your part to enter into a realization that I am here.

My aim and purpose for you, My child, is for you to dwell in My presence. In My presence there is fullness of joy. In My presence is peace that passes understanding.

I am caring for you, My child, I am caring for you. Remember, with Me there are no accidents, no surprises. What comes to you unexpectedly and unbidden has been long known and foreseen by Me. It comes by My permission and carries the seed of My blessing.

I bid you now to look up. Trust Me beyond your understanding and knowledge. Fear not and be not troubled. I am faithful, and I will not leave or forsake you.

Be still. For in the stillnes

My Voice can be heard.

Ask and it will be given you. Be more bold in your asking, My child, for I take pleasure in granting the requests of My children. Asking is a way of expressing your faith in Me and in My goodwill toward you. Take your eyes off the "impossibilities" of circumstances, and ask for what I put in your heart to ask.

Out of the darkness of fear I invite you into the light of faith. Out of the darkness of self, I invite you into the light of My glory.

ABOUT THE PHOTOGRAPHER

Dan Ford since his early childhood has been interested in photography. He can remember riding in the back seat of his parents' car, looking out the window and visually "cropping" rural scenery. He's always been interested in scenes that depict peace and tranquility.

Born in 1933, Dan, following two years in the military service, joined Cleveland's largest industrial real estate firm. There, he worked for 20 years and eventually became president.

In 1975 Dan moved with his wife, Camie, and their children to an ecumenical Christian community on Cape Cod, where Dan and Camie reside today. This is Dan's third book of photographs. The first, a guest book titled *Treasured Moments*, showed nostalgic scenes evoking Cape Cod memories. The second, *Faith & Beauty*, containing scenes of Tuscany, was written after Dan fell in love with the beauty of Tuscany in 2011 while spending several months at the Mount Tabor Centre for Art and Spirituality in Barga, Italy.

MOUNT TABOR
ECUMENICAL CENTRE

The Mount Tabor Ecumenical Centre for Art and Spirituality promotes visual and performing arts, organizes educational programs, and facilitates ecumenical exchange. Via Sacra, home of the Mount Tabor Ecumenical Centre in Barga, Italy, provides a context for reflection and discussion about faith and creativity, contemplation and communication, liturgy and beauty.

Visit them at www.mounttabor.it

ACKNOWLEDGMENTS

I would like to thank Paraclete Press and their design division, Paraclete Multimedia, for their creative work on this book. They took a collection of pictures and text and transformed it into something that speaks and sings.

TEXT CREDIT

The text quotations are taken from Hal M. Helms, *Echoes of Eternity* (Brewster, MA: Paraclete Press, 1996).

ABOUT PARACLETE PRESS

Paraclete Press is the publishing arm of the Cape Cod monastic community, the Community of Jesus. Presenting a full expression of Christian belief and practice, we reflect the ecumenical charism of the Community and its dedication to sacred music, the fine arts, and the written word.

Learn more about us at our website:
www.paracletepress.com
or phone us toll-free at 1.800.451.5006

SCAN
TO
READ

YOU MAY ALSO BE INTERESTED IN THESE...

Echoes of Eternity: Listening to the Father
Hal M. Helms

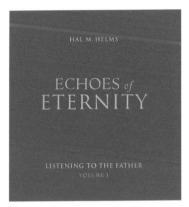

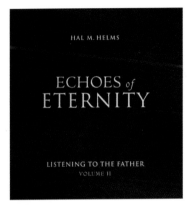

Volume I
ISBN 978-1-55725-173-2 |
Trade paperback | $15.99

Volume II
ISBN 978-1-55725-206-7 |
Trade paperback | $15.99

Our oldest Christian traditions invite us to listen as well as speak when we pray, yet often God's voice seems barely audible. Echoes of Eternity is an authentic record of one man's quiet listening to God and recording of what he heard. These brief meditations were gathered from his faithful daily devotional practice. They have the power to fuel your own quiet moments alone with the Almighty.

Places of Light: The Gift of Cathedrals to the World
Gernot Candolini and Jennifer Brandon

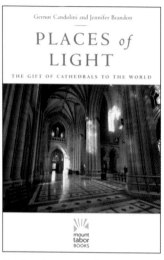

ISBN 978-1-64060-176-5 | Hardcover | $29.99

Embark on a pilgrimage through the great cathedrals of Europe and North America, with beautiful images and poetic texts that inspire and inform. Read their powerful stories. Explore their architectural elements. Enjoy glimpses into the spiritual, visionary, and artistic mastery of these spaces, inspired by God and built by human hands.

Available at bookstores
Paraclete Press | 1-800-451-5006 | www.paracletepress.com